Other Titles by the Authors of This Book

Gabriel Ricard

Ludicrous Split 2 (Back of the Class Press, 2023)
Benny the Haunted Toymaker Grows Up (Moran Press, 2021)
The Oddities on Saturday Night (Moran Press, 2020)
Ludicrous Split (Alien Buddha Press, 2018)
Love and Quarters (Moran Press, 2018)
Bondage Night (Moran Press, 2017)
Clouds of Hungry Dogs (Kleft Jaw Press, 2015)

Daniel W. Wright

From Obscurity to Oblivion: Collected Poems 2008-2017 (Spartan Press, 2022)
Love Letters from the Underground (Spartan Press, 2021)
Brian Epstein Died for You (Spartan Press, 2020)
Rodeo of the Soul (Spartan Press, 2019)

Tonight's Main Event

Poems by Gabriel Ricard and Daniel W. Wright

Liquid Lunch Press

To Brett
Enjoy the book!
Dan W. Wright

Liquid Lunch Press
Los Angeles, CA

Liquid Lunch Press

Copyright © Gabriel Ricard & Daniel W. Wright, 2024
First Edition: 1 3 5 7 9 10 8 6 4 2
ISBN: 978-1-958182-70-3

Cover Art by Brandon Barnes
Author photos: Caitlin MacKenna, Gabriel Ricard
All rights reserved. No part of this publication may be reproduced or transmitted in any form or by any means, electronic or mechanical, including photocopying, recording or by info retrieval system, without prior written permission from the author.

Acknowledgements:

The authors would like to acknowledge the following people:

Brian Zane for being kind enough to contribute a blurb for this book.

The authors also wish to acknowledge the crew of WrestleTalk, Alex Queen of the Ring, Kim Justice, and Wrestling Bios as being some of the best pro wrestling critics and reviewers in the game today.

Both authors would like to thank the friends and family who not only helped them become fans, but who went to shows with them and cheered until they were hoarse along with us.

Dan and Gabe wish to give a huge thanks to Jason Ryberg, who helped this book cross the finish line.

Table of Contents:

"Gababout" Gabriel Ricard

The 1997 Slammy Awards / 1
WrestleMania V / 5
PWI in the 90s / 9
Bad News Allen / 13
King of the Ring 1998 / 15
Interviewing Bret 'Hitman' Hart / 19
WrestleMania 28 (And the Slow Death of Fandom) / 24
The Mark Prime Shoot Interview Highlights
    Part 1: Introductions / 30
Mark Prime Shoot Interview Highlights,
    Part Two: The Early Days / 34
Mark Prime Shoot Interview Highlights,
    Part Three: The 1984 Push / 37
Mark Prime Shoot Interview Highlights,
    Part Four: Finances / 40
Mark Prime Shoot Interview Highlights,
    Part Five: Summer Clash '91 / 43
Mark Prime Shoot Interview Highlights,
    Part Six: Life's Amazing Journey Continues / 46
Mark Prime Shoot Interview Highlights,
    Part Seven: The Heart of a Champion Never Dies / 48
The Endless Hall of Fame Discourse / 52
Vince McMahon and Henry Kissinger / 55
Profilin at the Airport / 59

A Brief History of Women's Wrestling or the Slow
    Evolution of the Commercial Revolution / 64
The Standard Beast / 68
There Will Never be a Trainwreck Quite Like TNA / 73
The Rowdy One, Forever / 77

Dan "The Man" Wright

Guilty Pleasure / 87
Still Real to Me / 88
Heel Turn / 90
Von Erich Therapy / 92
Earn Your Stripes / 94
Get the Match in the Ring / 96
Walk That Aisle / 98
Hailing from Parts Unknown / 101
The Battle of the Bite / 102
Road Warriors / 104
No Holds Barred Grudge Match / 105
Austin vs McMahon / 106
Thunderlips / 108
Charlie Brown from Outta Town / 111
Satanic Sunshine / 113
Eleven Hours to Oklahoma City / 115
Black Star / 116
Acknowledge Him / 117
Million Dollar Body and a Ten Cent Brain / 118

This Television Thing is Here to Stay / 119

Hitting That Sweet Spot / 120

A Night with Mad Dog / 122

The Hot Tag / 124

Mark Them / 126

Elegy for Frank Goodish / 128

Backyard Badasses / 129

Didn't They Used to… / 131

The Many Sins of Vince McMahon / 132

A Higher Tolerance / 136

The Scaffold Match or Fuck That Shit,
    You're Not Getting My Ass Up There / 137

Blind Man with a Gun / 139

Harley Race vs the Hell's Angel / 141

Robocop Saves the Day / 142

Oh, I Knew That Guy / 144

Fear and Loathing in a Dairy Queen Drive-Thru / 145

Memories of a Modern Wrestling Fan
    from St. Louis / 146

The Bucks Gotta Stop Somewhere / 148

Got Your Nose / 149

Dedicated to the Memory of Katie Vick / 151

Exit Light, Enter Night / 153

Hate's a Hell of a Motivator / 154

When the Well Runs Dry / 156

Another Monday Night / 158

The Sickness / 159

In This Corner…

Weighing in tonight at 250 pounds!

From Orlando, Florida!!!

He is the author of several books, including *The Oddities on Saturday Night, Love and Quarters,* and *Benny the Haunted Toymaker Grows Up…*

He was formerly known as the laziest psychic on Long Island. One half of the tag team known as the Ludicrous Split!

"Gadabout" Gabriel Ricard!!!!!

Introduction

Amazing to me that in 25 years, I've never written poems about pro wrestling.

I've written fan fiction and other things when I was much younger, but never poems along these lines. I've broken everything down into three sections. One for my memories. One for random topics I felt like writing about. The third is a shoot interview with a fictional wrestler named Mark Prime.

When Dan Wright asked me if I was interested in doing this book with him, a lot of different ideas and anecdotes from my past suddenly came rushing to me. I realized as I started writing these that I had far more negative associations with this weird, amazing form of athletic entertainment than positive ones. This book doesn't change that, but it did go a long way towards making me understand why I stopped watching to a significant extent a few years ago.

But I'll always be a fan. It's hard to shake something that has been part of my life in some form or fashion for about 35 years. Like music and film, wrestling has been meaningful to my influences and dreams and ideas in ways that are hard, perhaps silly, to explain. No matter what, I can't seem to quit wrestling as a fan entirely.

Writing these poems reminded me of everything in wrestling that depresses me, and everything about wrestling that tires out my enthusiasm. At the same time, this book gave me more enthusiasm for what I do love about this sport than I've felt in quite possibly a full decade. I've exercised through writing some of the things about pro wrestling that annoy or sadden me, particularly most wrestling fans. What's left is a book I'm very proud of about a subject I'm glad has been part of my life.

Wrestling is surreal, heroic, ridiculous, dangerous, and ultimately something that never fails to surprise me. It's still real to me dammit.

For Cara and Michael Troy Shelton Jr.

The 1997 Slammy Awards

I was having the best weekend of my very young life
on the night of March 21st, 1997.
The Slammy Awards were on,
and I remembered them from the year before,
but I didn't get to watch.

But things were different in 1997.
My parents were months away from a custody fight
with gallons of blood flipping back and forth
between them in Virginia and Ucluelet, British Columbia.
I wasn't a teenager yet, but I probably believed I was.

And maybe it worked.
Maybe that was why I got to join our downstairs neighbor,
a man in his 20s married and raising a child
with a 14-year-old girl,
for a road trip
to northern British Columbia.
Meaning a ferry ride
from Vancouver Island to the mainland.
Meaning coffee and snacks at gas stations whipped
to shreds by the fact that blizzards
are still very fucking possible in late March
in British Columbia.
Meaning neighborhoods
and homes I had never seen before.
People and small towns
I had never whirled past in cars driven by
the eternally compromised

and constantly optimistic men who could drink
and drive and drug
and drive and smoke weed
and drive all night
and almost *never,* ever hurt anyone.

All things important to an 11-year-old boy.
I guarantee it.
At least this one.

We were in whatever beautiful, hateful little town
this guy's family had lived and died in
for a bunch of margarine-sized generations.
That's why we were there.
One of his brothers
wanted to go to Vancouver Island for work.

So, we were going to spend a couple of days
with large people who didn't like each other
and said a lot of racist things while drinking heavily
and watching weird shit like SummerSlam '92,
or In Your House: Final Four,
or Re-Animator at 4 in the morning.

I was excited for every horrible
and amazing part of it.
Making me feel like a grownup
was as easy
as convincing me that WrestleMania 13,
to be held a couple of days after the Slammys,
was going to be the greatest WrestleMania of all time.

I wouldn't get to see WrestleMania 13 live,
but I was following the Bret Hart/Steve Austin feud
more intensely
than anything else,
even the nWo,
and the Slammys were better than nothing.
One of the guys in the room with me
swore The Undertaker
had been played by several people.
I said no way.
Some of them were planning
to watch WrestleMania on Sunday,
but I wouldn't be there.

I had to be back home by then.
Someone actually expected me
  to go to school by then.

Wrestling had become a big part of my life
at this point,
and there was no better place to watch it
than with a bunch of *really* cool guys
in a small, dark living room.
Filled with stains and the kind of alcohol
and cigarette smells
the loneliest and dumbest of us are nostalgic for.

Fast food leftovers from a bygone era.
Blankets on the furniture
because that was technically
a good way to make them new again.

You can instantly see this kind of living room
if you were ever there.
And why are we even talking about this?
What normal person remembers talking with adults
about Sable and Sunny
and the best guys in the ring
at that time,
as a memory of a childhood
spent on good things?

Who the fuck cares
about Owen Hart stealing a Slammy
to keep alive the greatest gimmick
I didn't appreciate at the time?

I guess I do.
I suppose I care about these things.

I still think about those guys
I watched the show with,
and about how wrestling felt cooler
than it ever had before,
which is embarrassing to admit now,
but then one of those guys said something racist
about the Japanese and held up a copy of a movie
I had never even heard about before
called Ghost in the Shell,
so I think it all evened out in the end.

WrestleMania V

If I'd watched wrestling before April 2nd, 1989,
I don't remember it. I'm just barely a child of the 80s.
I don't remember much between
1985 and 1987. I'm sure I had a great time being barely alive,
overwhelmed by everything. Already anxious.

But I remember when I fell in love with pro wrestling.
Some friend's house where I watched WrestleMania V,
held on a Sunday at Boardwalk Hall in Atlantic City,
New Jersey. That was a ways from Lake Cowichan, BC,
and even then
as a kid I wondered what these weird places
would be like to visit.

Even Atlantic City.

I wanted to go places,
even if I couldn't begin to comprehend
how I would get anywhere,
and maybe pro wrestling was one of the ways
I could travel to places that weren't school or home.

Or I was just four years old,
and it was just a lot of goddamn fun
to watch big men in colorful costumes
seemingly beat the shit out of each other.

It doesn't really matter
where I saw WrestleMania V,
but I do remember witnessing,

and that's the word
when you're a little kid
and suddenly become a wrestling fan,
"Macho Man" Randy Savage
and Hulk Hogan
squaring off for the WWF title,
and thinking that nothing
before in my life had been as exciting
as those two trying to destroy each other
with wild punches, leg drops, elbow smashes,
aggressive finger pointing.
Brawling outside the ring
in such an intense way that it was easy to sell a little kid
on the notion that all of this was very, very real.

Miss Elizabeth was impossible
not to have a crush on.
Even if you were a preschooler,
who didn't even know
what the fuck a crush meant.

Savage and Hogan looked like gods from a comic book
at a time when comic book movies
were rare
and rarely good.
The Hart Foundation
obliterated The Honky Tonk Man
and Greg "The Hammer" Valentine,
looking like badasses in pink and black
as some adult in the room
mentioned that Bret Hart was a Canadian
from near where I was born
in Alberta.

Even The Ultimate Warrior was cool back then.
So was Rick Rude,
looking like an action movie villain
who could snap a fistful of spines
and talk trash and look good doing it all.

Roddy Piper was a lunatic
who I was told
could kick anyone's ass.
I just thought he was really funny,
but there was also something different, almost scary
about a guy who would attack you with a fire extinguisher.

Was wrestling always like this?
Was it always this much fun?

My mom didn't want me to watch
because I was the kind of child
who wanted to recreate the things he saw on TV.
Fair enough,
but nothing was going to stop me
from watching more wrestling
after April 2nd, 1989.

I don't think I could have done better
for an introduction
than a bloated PPV at a hazy address,
probably in the kind of filthy
1975 suburban coziness
that seemed like every living room
I ever saw in Canada in the late 1980s.

The best memories are sometimes made
in small rooms where the furniture, carpet stains,
and bizarre ravings of an older person who is very sick
are constantly subject to change.

Where agitated, visually absurd gods
like Brutus Beefcake,
Tito Santana, or even ol' Hacksaw Jim Duggan,
made everything else around me
just a little duller.

Even in 1989, I didn't want to be in the same place
day after day

PWI in the 90s

I couldn't watch whatever I wanted
whenever I wanted,
so that's at least one of the really good things
about pro wrestling these days.

1996/1997 in Ucluelet, British Columbia.
We didn't even have a fucking video store, man.

Hard times indeed, Dusty, indeed.

Just a couple of bleak convenience stores
where you could make depressing conversation
with the miserable, comically indifferent clerks,
buy shitty candy,
or rent a tape from a staggering selection
of 60 or 70 titles. Wrestling was only sporadically included,
and no one I knew was going to invite me over
to a PPV anytime soon.

For a long time,
I couldn't watch Monday Night Raw or Nitro either.

Truly, a Dickensian fever dream. You bet.

At least I didn't have to read Pro Wrestling Illustrated
or Wrestling All-Stars by candlelight.
The Apter Mags in particular
keeping me aware of incredible wrestlers
I couldn't watch in companies
like ECW,

New Japan,
All-Japan,
and this doesn't even get us into the decades
of wrestling history that fascinated me
because I was a super cool kid who loved to read about
the accomplishments of the dead and their cultural weirdness
in foreign galaxies
like New York City, Memphis TN, London, England
or Tokyo, Japan.

I had to wait for eBay to be invented
before I could start finding
and reading the older magazines
from the 70s and 80s.
When I was living in small Canadian towns,
I devoured any pro wrestling I could find.
Even if it was just some crap VHS tape
where Mr. Perfect and The Texas Tornado
traded the Intercontinental Championship
in ten wretched minutes
at some forgotten house show.

I settled for references to eras that fascinated me
simply because they seemed profoundly different to my present.
The rare home video. The books I found at the library
that weren't even written by wrestling fans half the time.

Someday, I'd get to watch and read all this history
until I couldn't stand it for another second,
and I'd get the fuck off Vancouver Island while I was at it.

Kayfabe stories and fantastic photography
marked the Apter Mags,

with Pro Wrestling Illustrated
being the only one that was available to me.

Inside Wrestling and The Wrestler weren't around,
and I wouldn't get to read them
until I was a little older
and in a completely different country.

Back to Canada for a minute though,
and it's 1997.
I've just finished walking
seven miles home in the rain.
Yes, really.

My clothes were drenched.
My hair was dirty and wet.
I was still thinking about the kid
who called me a faggot at school.
Being a wrestling fan before The Attitude Era
could be draining and depressing.

My parents were fighting every single day.
Screaming.
I could get away
if I was willing to get bullied for a few hours
in our small neighborhood
seven miles outside Ucluelet.

Otherwise, I stayed home to stare at the rain,
write fantasy wrestling scenarios in notebooks,
or treat my siblings like shit.

My mom would disappear
into the internet for hours at a time.
My dad would go to work
for days at a time.

None of that mattered
when I got in
from that long walk home in the rain.

I've got the 1997 PWI 500 in my backpack.
Dean Malenko is number one?
How?
Why isn't it Austin? Bret?
Hell, what about Diamond Dallas Page?

I couldn't wait to find out.

I was going to take a long bath
in sarcastically heavenly peace,
and I was going to read
the 500 from cover to cover,
and I was going to be
the happiest wrestling fan ever.

Hoping there would be some mentions
of past PWI 500s,
since there was no way to read those yet.

Bad News Allen

In April or May 1997,
I saw Bad News Allen wrestle on an indie card
in Port Alberni, British Columbia. Tim Flowers
was on the same card. A legend in his own right,
but Tim never won a battle royal at WrestleMania IV.

Bad News was a long way from Trump Plaza
and the shittiest giant trophy in wrestling history.

He was a long way from Toronto, Canada,
and Rowdy Roddy Piper painted half-black
for some unfathomable reason.

I didn't really know what the wrestling business
could do to a lot of guys back then.
I thought then that he looked fat and old and sad
and like he didn't really want to wrestle anymore.

He still had that nasty look in his eye though,
and there were moments when his fists flew
that he was pretty cool again.
I liked him when I was a kid
because he was a tough black dude
who didn't take shit from anybody.
Not even a probably-hopefully-probably-not-racist Piper.

I was disappointed in his match that night.
Nine years removed from betraying Bret Hart
in the final moments

13

of WrestleMania IV's commitment
to making sure the entire roster had a spot.

Didn't even bother
to commit the conclusion of the match
or Bad News' opponent to memory.
I have no idea.

I wish I had watched that match a little older.
I wish I could have at least appreciated the effort.

A veteran of three WrestleManias.
One of the best to come out
of Calgary's Stampede Wrestling.
I appreciate him now as a brutal,
remorseless loner from an era
of cartoon cowardice or unhinged heroism.

That guy deserved better than some asshole kid.
Expecting him to be the same guy
he was almost a decade earlier.

In general, really,
Bad News Allen deserved
and still deserves more
than just being the name
I've drawn from pro wrestling's ocean
of relative obscurity.

King of the Ring 1998

The Attitude Era was in full force by June 1998.
I know that because I was there
to be awestruck by most of it,
before growing up to be pretty indifferent
when someone tells me
that I lived through the greatest era
in pro wrestling history.

Somehow, I doubt it,
but no one's going to pretend
there wasn't a time
when everything was relentless and thrilling and edgy
and wild and violent and childish and a lot of other words
that made it an imperative even at the time
to watch chaotic history unfold.

Even at thirteen,
I understood that I was living
through a period of excitement
for pro wrestling fans
on par with Hogan in the mid-80s,
and that if everything in wrestling
was exciting in some way,
then the actual exciting stuff
was beyond any universe of calm explanation.

You knew just like I did
when The Undertaker threw Mankind
off the Hell in the Cell

at King of the Ring
on June 28th, 1998
that you were watching
one of the most unreal and unforgettable moments
in the history of professional wrestling.

Some matches wind up being greater
than even the hyperbolic potential
of this ridiculous, amazing, and dangerous industry,
and Mankind vs. The Undertaker Part 38,
or whatever we were at by then,
is one we're still talking about
in that sort of sense
that only makes sense
to wrestling fans who probably need to get a life.

Which would be all of us obviously.

Mick Foley is still talking
about the unfathomable decisions
he and The Undertaker made
on that blistering summer night in Pittsburgh.
This is still a very important story for so many people.

I'm not disagreeing with that importance or value.
Don't misunderstand me.

I remember watching it
in a clichéd-Tom-Waits-song motel room
with pay per view access,
because I lived alone with my dad
during the divorce and refused
to sleep in the car.

All because
he wouldn't settle for renting a home
that couldn't accommodate the kids
he thought he was going to win in the custody dustup.

That world was crushed by the sheer will
of the intangible enthusiasm
I could get from watching a copy of a copy
of WCW Uncensored '96,
let alone one of the biggest WWF pay-per-view events of the year.

Wrestling could distract me from anything in those days.

I actually screamed when Mick Foley
was thrown off the roof of the cell,
sailing through the sweaty, stifling air for an eternity
of stories and recollections. And somehow knowing
that even the more dangerous and violent moments
that would come later in wrestling history
just didn't hit
quite like Hell in the Cell at KOTR 1998.

I became an even bigger Mankind fan that night.
Wishing I could be there in the stunned and shocked crowd.
Wishing I could be in Pittsburgh.
Wishing I could be anywhere in the state of Pennsylvania, really.

Wishing I was anywhere else in the world,
even laying on the table
as Foley came crashing down
from the photogenic heavens,
if it meant leaving my miserable, desperate father
behind in that crime scene motel.

Pro wrestling made it easy and essential
to forget where I was,
or even where I might be going the next day.

And I'm still a Mick Foley fan.
Had a nice meet and greet with him and Noelle Foley
when Mick was exhausted and ready to go home,
but was very nice nonetheless,
on a delirious, hot August day in 2017.

It would have been weird to tell him where I watched *Hell in a Cell*,
(you can just say those words and most people
will choose The Undertaker vs. Mankind out of the dozens
of Hell in a Cell matches we've seen at this point),
but for some reason I really, really wanted to.

Interviewing Bret "The Hitman" Hart

I got to interview one of my wrestling heroes in 2008.

I've been a Bret Hart fan since I was 7 or 8 years old,
and it started because I just thought the jacket and the
sunglasses were cool.
But especially the tights.

No one else wore pink and black.
At least no one like Bret Hart did,
and sometimes it's enough
when you're a little kid
to throw on some rad tights
to throw down some realistic haymakers
at Mr. Perfect.

When you're eight,
it's impressive when someone wins
the WWF Intercontinental Championship
from someone as tough as Rowdy Roddy Piper.
I loved the jacket,
the music,
the realistic good guy persona,
the hair,
the elbow from the second rope,
again, the way he punched guys,
the Sharpshooter,
the sunglasses,
the fact that every match
he had was just really fun to watch
and care about.

Even a match with Virgil.
Or The Berserker.

A little more intense
in everything he said and did
than anyone else at the time.
He was relatively quiet,
but everything he said and did
had weight behind it.

Bret Hart and Steve Austin
had the greatest feud of all time.
I might be a semi-functional adult,
but I also might be willing to fight you
if you don't agree.

Bret Hart vs. Steve Austin
from November 1996 to July 1997
is the greatest period of time in wrestling
I have ever experienced as a fan.

If we're talking about
top ten
greatest of all time
lifetime contenders
for a discussion wrestling fans will come back
from the literal dead to participate in,
Bret Hart is my number one.

Certainly in 2008
when he agreed to a phone interview
with me, some kid who was still trying
to make a career

out of being the kind of writer
who rarely made money,

but who at least had fun.

I didn't make anything from interviewing Bret
and tying that into a review of The Wrestler,
a good movie that once again
put pro wrestling in the mainstream
in a fairly depressing way.
I just got to talk to one of my heroes
for over two hours.

I wanted to tell him about the couple of times
I got to be involved in something
vaguely resembling a wrestling business.
Although I had been exaggerating
those stories for so long
by that point it was probably best I didn't.
Self-humiliation flashbacks follow my dreams
and waking thoughts
like a pulse that wants to drop my enthusiasm
for life so far
it gives the mole people in the earth's core
fucking anxiety.

For example?
I still think it was stupid to tell him

that my brother Owen
was named after Owen Hart.
Technically true,
because I suggested it to my parents in the car

while reading a story about Owen Hart
possibly crippling Dan Severn
in (as always) Pro Wrestling Illustrated,
and my mom and her future fourth husband liked it.

But I'm sure I sounded like a weirdo.
No one wants to be another creepy wrestling fan.
At least I didn't.
Despite being very fucking weird
every fucking day.
I never wanted to admit it.

Living in the shadow
of the IT'S STILL REAL TO ME DAMMIT guy
apparently gave me the kind of PTSD
that only damages the brain if you choose to believe
the delusions you inhabit to coast safely through the pointless
days and weeks and months and-and-and

(losing focus
because this story is a real mixed bag for me
and I don't like thinking about it
for a variety of reasons)

And then I left a half-dozen messages
On the answering machine
of Bret's publicist
when he never sent back the copy
of his autobiography
I paid to have signed and returned.
The cringe of being so relentless
about a stupid book
still approaches me to this day.

Whenever I'm gullible enough
to think I can handle life's annoyances
like that functional adult sleepcore
TV commercial dream spokesperson
we were trying to conjure up earlier.

It's hard to enjoy things, I guess.

Even honest-to-fucking-God Owen Hart stories
from the honest-to-fucking-Hitman
the Excellence of Execution.

WrestleMania 28 (And the Slow Death of Fandom)

I was so hung over on April 1st 2012.
In the hours before WrestleMania 28 came and went
on to the oblivion of short-term memories
that live forever in the shittiest archives,
I was still apologizing to friends
in Smithfield, Virginia
who had put me up and were putting up with me.
I had gotten a little silly the night before, and there was
a lot of concern and frustration flying around the kitchen.
I steadied myself with cigarettes and coffee and secret beers
and tried to make sense of the universe
just enough to actually feel remorse for what I'd done.

My friends were pissed.
What if their kids had seen me like that?
Fair enough. Fair enough.
Goddamn my head was pounding
 to the rhythm of keeping me spiritually centered
on personal and professional dehydration.

Couldn't hold my liquor again.
It would be embarrassing
for everyone by association if it hadn't shifted
to something scarier than that
because it can go any one of six thousand ways with
someone who drinks because they're bored and uncomfortable.
That routine of traveling just to be lonely somewhere else.
Or passively watching things around you change.
Regardless of your participation in them.

I wasn't sorry so much as I was just exhausted
and waiting for Danny T to come pick me up
for the WrestleMania 28 watch party.
I didn't really care
if they were upset.
I was a little pissed off with myself
for drinking so much Kahlua and bourbon.

Not together.
I wasn't a fucking weirdo.

WrestleMania 28 was a strange one in retrospect.

Going to a watch party seems strange in retrospect, too.

It's hard to imagine these days watching anything with anyone.
I'm only half-kidding,
and I'd like to pretend
that's a sign of maturity,
and not someone who turned
Splendid Isolation
into a moral code.

Sheamus beat Daniel Bryan in eighteen seconds
for the World Heavyweight Championship.
I didn't have the diligence and discipline
being a true wrestling fan demands,
since there's roughly 800 hours of content
to consume and half-chew weekly,
but even I thought it was kind of fucking stupid
to have a potential three-or-maybe-four-star classic
wrap up in the time it took me

to hope some boneless wings and vodka gummy bears
would magically make me stop sweating.

It was hard to stop feeling so clammy.
White, damp death wrapping around the skin
so tight until it shoots you out the door
for an optimistic cigarette
and some fresh April Virginia Beach humidity.
It was hard to be charming to a girl
I immediately liked in between barely memorable showdowns
between Randy Orton and Kane
and The Big Show and Cody Rhodes.

What's the point of all this?
I wanted to go home.
I didn't like the people I was watching the show with.
This was Danny T's crowd.
I'm sure it still is even though he's been dead
for almost a decade now.
Pro Wrestling isn't very social
if you hate the internet
and still remember all the people who called you queer
for so long you decided to just keep your interests
to your own fucking self.

I just didn't care about wrestling the way I used to.

Not even Undertaker/Triple H III could do it for me,
although I've since rewatched this match
and like it a lot more than I did the first time.
The participants went hard,
throwing Shawn Michaels into the mix

to create a different sort of drama
from the last two encounters.
It mostly worked.

The End of an Era.
Well, one of the ends anyway.
It was a physical, emotionally charged match.
Especially with Shawn Michaels playing referee.
Three of my childhood favorites
proving they could still keep up with the younger talent,
who deserved their spot just as much.

It was fine.
I think that might have been the night I realized
that I would become someone
who could go on for hours
about the long-gone legends and classics
of 1989, 1997, 1977, 2007,
or whatever the case might be,
but who just didn't want to keep up
with the shadow army death march
of pop culture that comes and goes
like a sky city of robotripping UFOs.

Nostalgia and depression.
Nostalgia but make it different.
No, that's too different, and I don't know why
you hate the fun of the past
constantly informing your future.

Nothing ages you
quite like the pace of the wrestling business

or the memories of people
who hate that they aren't eleven anymore.

Undertaker won.
He'd keep the streak going for a few more years.
Wrestling far longer than he ever should have.
There's a lot of that in wrestling.
If they even live that long to begin with.

And somehow,
despite all of this,
I still feel like I had a good time at the watch party.
All things roughly considered
for bleak-but-vaguely-wholesome posterity.

I'm still watching wrestling to some degree.

Like most of you,
I don't know how to fully walk away
from the parts of my childhood
that don't particularly appeal to me anymore,
but I chase and chase and chase
to find the phantom of a pleasing memory.

Nevertheless.

Wrestling remains one of my favorite ways
to trap myself in unrealistic expectations
and glassy portraits
of all the fun
I allegedly used to have.

But it's not all bad.
It's not wholesale bitterness.

Sometimes,
on the kind of night
where Terry Funk might suddenly wrestle
one more match
one more time
for the umpteenth time,
or when I remember the top-to-bottom brilliance
of WrestleMania X-7
or any 1980s Midnight Express variation,
I forget all of that bullshit
and just have a good time.

The Mark Prime Shoot Interview Highlights
Part 1: Introductions

My name is Mark Prime,
and that's been my name in the ring for over 30 years.

I legally changed it 10 years ago
to celebrate 5 years of sobriety. That didn't last much longer,
but Mark Prime will always be better than Mark Cartuna.

There's something fortunate about my name, I guess.
I know a lot of guys who went through their careers
with a new handle every couple of years because it just wasn't
quite clicking.

Or no one really cared,
so you could just be whoever,
when the time came to evolve
to stay in the lower middle
of the bottom of the industry.

Sometimes,
that feels like where I've spent most of my career, too,
but at least I've managed to keep my name.

There's value in it.
I've wrestled everywhere.
I've won a thousand matches.
If I had to guess.
But I've lost a few hundred, too.

There are even people
who remember me.
Some fans in Nagasaki.
A Facebook page someone started in Mexico City
with 3,298 members and counting.

People who love the 90s love my ass.
I'm big shit in a few dozen hometowns.

There might even be a Hall of Fame spot
with my name on it.
If anyone ever actually bothers to build one, I guess.

There's award dinners
in depressing places like upstate New York.
There's a company
that has a ceremony every year,
inducting guys who didn't even wrestle for them,
and ignoring anyone who thinks it might be kind of cool
if there was an actual monument of some kind to go
with the speeches.

I wrestled for those guys. A lot.
Remember when I was on a big deal on TV?
Remember when I was a tag team champion
with a few million eyes
on the *PRIME* of my career? Heh. I do.

I got a run with another belt.

Remember the Dog Collar Match?
Remember the main event of Summer Clash '91?

Top of the fucking midcard, man.
That was exciting for a while.

I remember. They haven't called me yet.

If they do, I might tell them I'm too busy
doing a tour of the young and the restless and the old
and the heartless over in Australia.
Then some dates in Memphis.
An autograph show in New Jersey after that.
Maybe a couple of shows
for an upstart in Winnipeg.

Wouldn't that be a fucking trip.
I miss Canada.

I'd probably answer the phone,
being honest.

I'm ready to talk about where I've been,
and it would be nice if a few thousand more people
cared about that,
and then they got together and made sure
everyone else paid attention.

I know all about social media.

My wife says it's time to start planning for the future,
which you can apparently still do at 61.

Getting older. What a shit show.
You care about the dumbest nonsense
all of a sudden.

You wonder if the blood and the injuries
and the grudges and the bad food
and amazing tequila
were worth the trouble.

Probably was.

What else should I have done
for my 15th birthday,
and then for a few decades after that?

I guess we're going to answer that eventually.

I guess I'm ready to answer all of your questions.
If you got any worth a damn.

Mark Prime Shoot Interview Highlights Part 2: The Early Days

It's true in my opinion that the kids wrestling today
just don't know how easy they have it sometimes.

Someone told me recently
that a trainer got fired
from Global Wrestling Empire last month
because they screamed at some trainee
until he broke down in tears.

Imagine if that kid had been
in Gene Lewis' camp
back in the 80s.
Like I was.

4 AM. Every day. Every fucking day.
We're running
from one end of that horrible fucking town
in Florida to the other. Shinjiro Murakami stretching your guts
from your asshole up over the top of your head,
after Gene made you do a few hundred pushups.

Screaming in that deep Canadian accent of his
every step of the way. Sure, guys broke down sometimes.
Not me,
but other dudes did in private sometimes.
And that's just the thing.
In private.

You swallowed your pain, had a few beers,
and got up again in the morning
to hope you lived long enough
to see if you could steal the show
in front of twenty-two people in Council Grove.

Which I did.
I took the worst abuse you can imagine
for almost a year,
before I even stepped in the ring.
Thundro the Giant pinned me
in forty-two seconds in my first match.
Ever see it?
Broke two of my ribs and gave me a concussion,
and it was a fuckin honor
to prove I was willing to come back next week
and do it all again.

That's how men were made back then.
I guess that's not the way it's done anymore.

Shame.
Maybe that's why the current crop
of kick-happy jobbers, and whorebags,
and flat fucking so-called men who'd rather
hang out on TikTok than go to the gym,
are just not something I feel like watching on TV.

I told you. I know social media.

God save us all, brother,
because seriously,

seriously, dude,
who cries because someone yells at you?
Whatever. We're not here to talk about
what's wrong with wrestling these days.

We're here to talk about that good, sweet shit.
How it only took me a couple of years
in dying territories and local outdoor flea markets,
before I went to Japan
and really made some fuckin noise.

Gene later called me the best wrestler he ever trained.
Not a lot of people know that.

I think he meant it, too.

Gene didn't just say that shit to anyone
when he was sober and his kids were talking to him again.

Mark Prime Shoot Interview Highlights Part 3: The 1984 Push

You want to know what it was like
at the height of everything in the 80s?

Well, I wish I'd saved some fucking money,
that's for sure,
but maybe I wouldn't be all that entertaining
to your audience
if I had.

No one wants to hear from the guys who retired with millions.
All 38 of them. The 9 soldiers with Sainthood
and then whoever's left. Not me anyway. Anyway–

Buying boats, coke,
and some guitars I forgot to learn to play.
Women who were a lot sweeter than the ring rats,
and no one ever talks about how the pussy got better
when wrestling went mainstream.

When it's fun, it's fun,
and sometimes you get lucky and it doesn't run out.

I liked spending big and as fast as possible.
Get a little anxious about finances,
before turning the faucet on again.

Even after I had kids.

I didn't have a lot of free time back then,
wrestling 280 to 340 dates a year for Global,
and I was there for a while, making good fucking money, too,
so why not try to break the monotony in a meaningful way.

No way these kids now could handle 300 dates a year.
Especially these fucking perverts and all this stupid shit
about gender and fairness and goddamn I can't even imagine
wrestling a man with a cunt who says he's still a man.

Trying lacing up my boots.

But anyway.
Yeah, we worked hard back then. That's my point.
Everyone was making money. Crusher Morgan, Thundro the Giant,
and Mick Kash were making millions.

Even a guy at the top of the middle like me benefitted.
I joined in January '84,
and by the end of the year,
Gary and the rest of the bookers
were talking about a bigger push for me. Maybe a program
with Morgan.

I was living a half-dozen dreams in one clusterfuck
of an afternoon.
You'll never know just how fucking amazing it was.

I was up for anything.
It was easy to be.
Even when you got hurt.

You just did what you had to do,
went on to the next town,
and thanked the veterans for taking you out to get drunk
at the end of another show where you knew
your turn was finally coming up.

Everything was picking up big lungfuls of momentum, man!

Maybe too fast,
but fuck it,
you may as well keep up and have fun,
until the ex-wives outnumber the kids
who grow up to become boring-ass sober dorks
and cops and shit.

Dangerous Diamond Tate used to tell me that.
Until he passed away in '97 from an enlarged heart.

They don't make managers like that anymore.

Mark Prime Shoot Interview Highlights Part 4: Finances

Let me be clear though. I'm not "broke" broke.
I've got some money. Between the autograph shows,
a match here and there,
and the home security business I do some consulting work for,
I'm not some Mickey Rourke sad story bullshit.

I've got a fucking house. Okay?

Okay.

But yeah,
If I had been maybe paid a little more,
maybe been a little smarter sometimes,
maybe, sure, maybe,
I'd have a couple million in the bank.
You bet.
Maybe.

Before he died at 52 from an enlarged heart,
Big Sid Needles used to tell me
that we were going to
retire and that he'd take care of me
because he understood the markets and all that shit.
He was good about investments.

You know how much he had
when he fell over at his gym,
getting ready for that big comeback match in Japan
with King Kayashi Studd?

800K. That's what he told me.
Not bad. Not bad at all.

I'd settle for having
my Bloody Brawl III payday again.
Me and Cowboy Brett Blair.
Dog Collar Match.
The Garden wasn't ready for us
to beat the living SHIT out of each other
for twenty-three and a half fucking minutes.
They told us we could go hard,
but not as hard as we had been
in Florida a few years back
before Brett and I both headed north
roundabout the same time.

There was a little heat from management, yeah.
Heh.

But it was worth it.
We were still pretty young.
We could still go.
The highways didn't have a prayer
at wearing us down,
and you could get away with so, so much
if you were a star or close enough.

I think I was a star more years than not, buddy.
What do you think?

Anyway,
I got 80, 000 for that one night.

Un-fucking-real, man.
Since you're a fucking nerd,
you know what happened after that.
I'm kidding!
I'm kidding!
You kids are so fucking sensitive now!

But yeah.
The motorcycle was the most expensive one
in the shop.
That's my bad I guess.
Between that and the medical bills
for the accident,
I think that money went the way
of the piledriver
in about forty-eight hours.

Forty-eight hours.

Just fucking imagine that.
I know I do.

Mark Prime's Shoot Interview Highlights Part 5: Summer Clash '91

I guess Summer Clash '91 was the biggest night of my career.

I don't really see it that way,
but people like you sure seem to think it was my best match.
It's a big one, yeah, but I don't know if I'd call it
the best match of my career, and I guess. Well.

The fuck are you trying to say?
You saying I didn't do anything worth a shit after that?
You know that was a long ways back, right?

Maybe I haven't even fucking peaked yet.
Huh, smartass.

I'm kidding. Calm down.
You don't have to stop recording.

Maybe I'm stalling.
Maybe I'm not a badass
when it comes to talking about a match
I've rambled about more than any other.
How many of these fucking interviews
do you think I've done about this and only this?

Not even the first or last time
I was in the main event
Wasn't the first or last time
I challenged for the World Heavyweight Title, either.

So what the fuck?

What is it with you fucking nerds
and this goddamned match?

Crusher was injured as shit and hungover.
I broke a finger on that son of a bitch cage door.

We just beat the hell out of each other
for thirty minutes.
I was so tired in those days,
I stopped trying to tell the difference
between the days of the week.
If Crusher talked to me about the match
beforehand, I don't fucking remember anymore.

Took nine chair shots to the head right?
That's the number right?

I'll take your goddamn word for it.

Then he pinned me.
What the fuck ever, man.

I was the fifth choice anyway.
Mick Kash was hurt.
"Rock and Roll" Heavyweight Hartigan
had been arrested at the Canadian border
a month earlier.

People remember this drizzling shit match
because the rest of the card was a fucking nuclear holocaust.

That bullshit women's title match?
The Texas Tornado match
with a DQ finish?

A first blood match where both guys bleed
in the first five fucking minutes?

Tell me I'm fucking wrong!

I don't remember much more than that,
and I'd rather you get me some more fucking beer
if you're going to actually expect me to remember
this fucking bullshit one more fucking time.

I keep telling people the matches me and Crusher
had in Japan
five years earlier were the real classics,
but no one listens
and no one fucking cares.

I'm done with this shit.

Next fucking question.

Hurry
the
fuck
UP.

Mark Prime's Shoot Interview Highlights Part 6: Life's Amazing Journey Continues

I was ready for a change.
I don't care what anyone says about some drug test.

I failed the test but what the fuck. Everyone failed
those tests back when. If you even had to take one
to begin with. They were mad at me. Just fucking pissed
like a bunch of babies, because I decided it was time
to renegotiate, before I went out there to drop the TV title
to that fucking jellyfish Jake Steele. Handsome Hero.
Bullfuckingshit.

What do you mean you won't run out for more beer?
Just take it out the money
you're paying me for the shoot.

Fuck you.
That was not the whole goddamned amount.
That's called an advance,
you fucking queer bait,
an ADVANCE.

They paid me 10K in Atlantic City
to drop the belt.
Fucking losers.
The booking whims
of a goddamn retard.
You're fucking me around
right now.

Turn off the motherfucking camera.
Fuck you.

I'm not fucking drunk.
I outdrank Jerry Streets
before you were born, peckerhead.

They fucked me over
like a paid whore
with the drug test
cause I knew just what the fuck
I was worth back then.

More than those parasites
ever realized.

You can be sure of that.
You better be sure of that.

Mexico was a good move
for me anyway.
Getting away from the domestic assault bullshit.
Getting away from a schedule
that turns good men into dog food.

I made so much fucking money.
That's a country that knows how to treat talent.

Mark Prime's Shoot Interview Highlights Part 7: The Heart of a Champion Never Dies

Fuck this.
Sell it on the internet.
Whatever.

You got until these two beers are finished,
and then I'm fucking out of here,
and you're lucky my hip is fucked
or I'd be kicking the bitch out of somebody right here
and right now, man.
You fucking believe it, dude.

The new generation?
A bunch of chicks.
Kicking.
Playing on their phones.

Do wrestlers even throw punches anymore?
Are you allowed to say
anything MEAN about your opponent?

Someone on my Twitter said
it's just woke garbage.
Whatever that means.
It's exhausting.
Everyone tires me out.

These kids today are a joke.
A sarcastic impression of a joke.

They'd rather suck dick at a police protest
then learn how to slow down
and actually work a half-decent match.
Ask me something else.
The kids are fucked UP.

The bus crash outside London
on my last European tour with the company?
You know exactly what the fuck I'll say to that.
Next question.

Winning the tag belts for the first time?
Who the fuck remembers tag teams anyway?
Losers.

Next question.
Next fucking question.
Let's go.
What've you got?

Best crowds?
The ones with pussy and free drinks
at the hotel bar later.

The Scaffold Match in '88?
I was so fucking coked out I couldn't tell you
if that even really happened.
It did?
Well whoop-dee-fucking-shit, brother.

Do I miss being in the ring?
I haven't fucking left yet.

49

My hip might be fucked
but people are not going to stop paying to see me.

And I still have shit to pay for.

No, I don't get to wrestle as much as I used to.

I'm adjusting.
That's a word I learned recently.
I'm ad-just-ing.

Health insurance.
Health insurance would be nice.
Another year near to the middle of the top please.

Tell my loser kids their dad is sick.
Fuck you, I don't need to elaborate a shit thing, dude.

Goddamn. Please. Please. Please.
Let me do this shit again. Let me get it right
this one goddamn time.

No one's offering me a Legend's deal
And I'm FUCKING SICK OF IT.

NEXT FUCKING QUESTION.

We're done? Fuck. Fine.

Have fun never fucking a woman, dork.
Fuck your website. What the fuck is YouTube?
Fuck your "viewers."

Fuck you. Goodbye.

Make sure you leave in the part
where I'm free for bookings after March.

I will fucking phone your ass if you don't.

The Endless Hall of Fame Discourse

The Chris Benoit murder-suicide tragedy
was
in hindsight

probably my beginning of the end
of being a fan of pro wrestling.

But that's beside the point.

Chris Benoit is probably one of the ten best wrestlers
of my lifetime.
From Japan, to ECW, to WCW,
to WWE and the rest of a life spent collecting concussions
like some wrestlers collected ring rats or sorrowful stories
of loneliness and despair from the road.

For our entertainment,
and to prove that a "small" guy (5'11 is still pretty tall)
could be a big player
in a world of Hulk Hogans and Undertakers,
Chris Benoit experienced possibly dozens of instances
of brain trauma in a twenty-year career
that I don't think was ever not stiff chops
and visually breathtaking diving headbutts
off the top rope.

Some pointed out,
after he murdered
his wife Nancy and seven-year-old son Daniel,
that his brain damage put him about even
with an eighty-year-old Alzheimer's patient.

That's not a justification.
It's just probably the reality of constant physicality
and pretending we only learned about brain damage
a decade ago.

Benoit made choices.

That doesn't make what happened to him okay.
It doesn't make his murders okay either.
It's really all just one slow-moving mass
of chemicals and road signs
and dead bodies and a continent's worth
of haunted plastic
and everything else you would need
if you wanted to physically represent
one of the worst wrestling stories
you're ever going to hear.

And that's unfortunately
the only story that matters anymore.

Not the one about a 5'11 guy in a 6'6 industry
who sincerely beat the odds with nothing more
than just happening to be one of the most extraordinary athletes
to ever commit his body and soul to professional wrestling.

Not the one where that 5'11 miracle of force of will
stands before his family, his contemporaries, and his fans
on the night he's inducted into the WWE's Hall of Fame.

A tearful, grateful
legend who begins
by wishing his best friend

Eddie Guerrero
was there tonight.

Actually,
since we're dreaming lovely, horrible dreams,
let's say Eddie is still alive, too,
and let's say the Hall of Fame is a building
we're going to see
the next time we want to pretend

we're running away from our problems
by going on vacation.

But that story for Benoit died
when he killed his wife and son
in a mental state that can scarcely be comprehended,
but is seemingly not an issue
to former promoters like Paul Heyman.

Good thing Paul didn't allow
for chair shots to the head
in ECW right?

Anyway, Chris Benoit is dead,
and you can whine all you want
about the HoF, but nevertheless,
there are realities,
arguably even consequences,
for pro wrestling and Chris Benoit alike.

Sometimes your guy doesn't get to go
to the Hall of Fame.

Vince McMahon and Henry Kissinger

I haven't listened to it,
but apparently there's a podcast about bastards,
and there's a six-episode run
dedicated to Vince McMahon.

"Six episodes," someone on the internet said
with horrified astonishment.

Henry Kissinger got six episodes.

It's one of those rare times
when you can reasonably discuss
Henry Kissinger and Vincent Kennedy McMahon
in the same conversation.
I wonder how Vince feels about the show
calling him history's greatest monster.
Without listening to any of this,
I would assume they're being tongue-in-cheek.
Vince McMahon and Kissinger
could probably have a conversation
about being pragmatic
when it comes time to decide
if someone or something needs to be destroyed.

But obviously, Kissinger destroyed millions of people.
Literal millions.
Killed a lot a lot a lot a LOT of them,
but there's also
a lot a lot a LOT
of other ways to obliterate someone or something.

Anthony Bourdain was being kind
when he said he wanted to beat Kissinger to death
with his bare hands after visiting Cambodia.

Vince wasn't given the same resources
to run wild, brother,
so I guess we're at least on the timeline
where his family stays in wrestling
whether they want to or not.

But you have to wonder
what a man who beat a federal investigation
in the 90s would have done
with just a little more power.
Being a living god
in your multimillion-dollar fishbowl
will probably never be enough for him.
That can't help but be fascinating.

A genuinely important figure
in wrestling's history
who actually accomplished things,
unlike his WrestleMania host
and fellow rape enthusiast
Donald Trump.
So beloved
is the former
ECW World Heavyweight Champion
a couple million people
are gleeful to overlook
the horrendous things he did on the road
to change wrestling forever,

and then the horrendous things he did on the road
to take the WWF,

eventually WWE,
to heights his father
never dreamed of.

And then the things he did when he became lazy,
but somehow kept the same ambition and greed,
because there wasn't much left for him to do
by the dawn of a shameful new millennium.

More than enough
for six 90-minute episodes of a podcast,
even if you spend a long time
setting up the background
of the point every wrestling fan
is at least aware of.

The one where Vince McMahon
is probably worse than anyone imagined.
Even if someone doesn't want to admit it,
they know.
When the stories accumulate,
even from your friends,
it almost always means the awful truth
you pretend isn't important.

But no,
probably not as evil as Kissinger.

But yeah,
you can see the two of them getting along.

You can see some shared qualities, sure.

Although it should be said
that while I don't know

if Vince McMahon would have bombed Cambodia,
at the bottom of the bottomless Hell
that was somehow also the sickening precipice
of the Vietnam War,
I do think Henry Kissinger
could have booked WrestleMania.

Henry probably would have kept the show going
after indirectly murdering Owen Hart.

And I think the XFL
would have gone the same way
for either of them.

Profilin at the Airport

It's 2016.
Ric Flair's drunk at the airport again.

Surprisingly youthful hair
stuck to his forehead again.
Nine A.M. again.
Japan again.
Minneapolis again.
2 AM in Puerto Rico again.
1991 again.
1983 again.
1975 again.

Not even the legends of nervous breakdowns
in the TSA line that starts in Raleigh
and goes all the way to London
and the rest of Europe can sweat as much
as this guy could on a bad day in 2016.

Or 2012.
Or 2005.

There's only one Ric Flair.
That's good and bad.
Extraordinary and tragicomedy Americana.

We're having this conversation. Again.
Again, he's one of a kind in any decade.

The greatest of all time in 1980 and 1992
and for a long while after that.

Still arguably among the best wrestlers
to lace up a pair of boots in 2003 or 2008
with steady, steady, impossibly steady hands.

Arguably because no one is as good
at fifty-eight
or seventy-three
as they were at thirty-two or forty-one,
but there also haven't been a lot of people
getting into the ring
at fifty-eight,
or sixty-two,
or seventy-three.

Never mind being half as good
as he used to be
on almost any of those occasions,
because that's still better
than a lot of wrestlers half his age.

And again, and of course,
there's only one Ric Flair in any of these decades.

Reports from the airport in Boston in 2016
were sketchy.
Somebody said something about a head injury.
Someone else said he'd been drinking
bloody marys since 2 AM.
Cheering on friends who had left him there hours ago.

Possibly years ago.
This is a man who lives in the past on a good day
in 2001, or 1999, or 2011,
or in a coma in 2018,
and a lot of us are quite okay with that.

There's probably worse things to be
than broke again.
Drunk at the airport again.
Living in the past again.
Wrestling again.
In 2022!
And at least that's probably because
he really wants to,
and not because of the being broke thing,
but because of that other thing where you live your gimmick
so hard your ex wives outnumber the times you pulled yourself
away from being a permanent universal laughingstock.

He wrestled his last match in 2022.
Maybe his last, but maybe not,
and he probably would even if it was easy to afford
the limos, the suits, the alimony,
the need to buy everyone a drink
because that's how friendships are made,
MEAN
WOO!
BY GOD
GENE,
WOOO!,
and it's getting harder and harder
to watch him pretend
1989 just wrapped up the other day.

But I'm still watching, still a fan,
and still hopeless
about pro wrestling nostalgia,
and the stillness inherent in understanding
that nothing makes you think
of an easier age and time
quite like Ric Flair.
He gets that better than anyone,
and has to live with the guy on top of that.

But he's still pushing forward.
We're still entertained.

Sue, it gets a little sadder every day,
but that's pro wrestling more often than not.

Either it's bleak, brief.
No one remembers you.

Or you're one of the greatest of all time
on any day or in any era,
and you get up every morning
because what else is there to do,
and you hope your legacy will be enough
for the good to outweigh the panic attacks,
snide comments,
sexual harassment accusations,
depression, poor business decisions
etc. etc. etc.

When someone finally comes to tell you
to go home to your rented mansion
and start making new plans.

Something where you don't have to bleed
like an Italian zombie movie anymore.

Or something where the future
finally finds you in the present
and keeps you there forever.

Whether you like it.
Or you don't like it.
Because diamonds are forever,
and so is Ric Flair.
Or so he hopes.

A Brief History of Women's Wrestling or the Slow Evolution of the Commercial Revolution

Or something less pretentious for the title,
but let's talk about the history of women's wrestling anyways.
When I was a kid,
there was Sherri Martel,
Alundra Blayze,
Bull Nakano,
Luna Vachon,
and that was pretty much
just about it.
Yeah, there were others,
but you were lucky in the 80s and 90s
to see maybe 10 minutes of women's wrestling
in a full calendar year
from the WWF or WCW. Or the NWA. Or the AWA.
Unless you went to Japan
or set yourself up for disappointment
with the LPWA or GLOW.

I was wrong to think women's wrestling
was never going to
get out
of 2006.

There were managers.
Miss Elizabeth.
Baby Doll.
Sunny.
Missy Hyatt.

Francine.
Dawn Marie.
Beulah.
Sherri
and Luna
and Alundra
(Madusa if you watched her
beat Paul Heyman's ass live on PPV in WCW)
all managed guys because there just wasn't enough
of an almost-complete void to go around.

But women's wrestling didn't really start to become a thing again
until the late 90s. WCW started and immediately disregarded
a World Women's Championship.
WWE brought it back
so Sable would have something to do
that didn't necessarily have to involve
actually being good at wrestling.
WWE kept the belt around
even after Sable left,
which could be considered better than nothing
but it was still
a jiggle jiggle slap and tickle kind of thing
for years.

And you were definitely gay,
just a big ol' homosexual,
if you thought that maybe it would be cooler
if the women could actually wrestle for more than three minutes.

It's hard not to romanticize Trish Stratus a little.

Elevating her division
didn't stop her from also being one of the most beautiful
people in modern wrestling history.
Not even Vince McMahon's gross fucking tongue
in her mouth was going to stop her.
Women's wrestling got better through legitimate determination.

But slowly.
It's really only been close to decent in North America
for about a decade and some change.
The socially conscious part of all this
that makes actual men bitch
like drunken baby pigs
is in knowing
that we've still got a long way to go.
Asuka. Becky Lynch. Awesome Kong.
Mickie James. Lita. Charlotte Flair. Rhea Ripley.

It's astonishing how many amazing women
make it so that we almost never have to mention that
piece of shit Fabulous Moolah
ever again.

But we've got a long way to go. Always right?
Progress that feels meager when you're forced to live through
the slow details of the routine of days that are simultaneously
too fast and too much of a slog to even think about until,
well, you don't have to anymore.

And speaking of time,
WWE needs to age this poem
with another all-women pay-per-view.

Amen.

And speaking of women and WWE,
God and science
protect Wendi Richter and Cyndi Lauper
while we're at it.
Amen.

At least they get to see women's wrestling finally mean something,

One of the few things
about the sport (entertainment)
that actually makes my cranky old ass happy,

While Moolah burns in the sort of hell
where they keep Mae Young's birthed hand
or every single dumb fucking HLA RAW segment.

Just like with the men,
or anyone else who gets into the ring,
you can lust after someone who also kicks a lot of ass.

Why can't it be both,
if you're into that kind of thing?

And I don't know who needs to hear this,
but it's also actually fine,
if they just
kick someone's ass.

The Standard Beast

Brock Lesner is one of those things
where I guess I'm just the asshole
who doesn't really get it.

2002 was a weird year for wrestling.
The Attitude Era was dying, wheezing,
and becoming an increasingly odd friend
to invite to a party where guys
like Lesner, John Cena, Batista,
and Randy Orton were poised to take over
from the likes of
Mick Foley,
The Rock,
and an increasingly unreliable
Stone Cold Steve Austin.

Lesner was and is an amazing physical sight.
You could have told me he was 7'10 and 800 pounds,
and I would have believed you on the strength
of his scowl and lack of neck alone.

This was a guy who at least looked like someone
who would kill a human being for shits and giggles,
and pro wrestling often has to work desperately hard
to even suggest that kind of authenticity.

And then he started wrestling,
and it didn't take me long to get bored
with yet another guy who did five or six things
reasonably well,

but that was apparently enough to become
The Next Big Thing ™.

Like I said,
I'm just the asshole
who doesn't really get it.

For every Brock Lesner match I enjoyed,
there were a half-dozen
that made me wish I'd watched something else.

I love old Hulk Hogan matches,
and it doesn't get more simplistic than that,
so like I said, again,
I'm just the asshole
who doesn't really get it.

Suplex. Repeat. Suplex. Rest hold.
Suplex. Paul Heyman is screaming again.

Did people really watch that shit
for 8+ years when he came back?

Sorry. Sorry.
Sorry.
Trying to be nice.

Let people
enjoy
things
even
if

they

suuuuuuuuuuuuck

And yeah,
there's more to wrestling than the main event,
but this is WWE we're talking about,
and they're very fond of making sure we remember
the main event players at any given point
during any given show.

When Brock disappeared for a dreamlike decade,
I decided to be stupid and hopeful
that he was gone for good.

Wrestling seemed to do just fine without him.

And then 2012 happened,
and Brock was back to conquer WWE again.

Squash match. Suplex City.
A sprawling metropolitan landscape where everything looks,
sounds, and functions the same for eternity.
Suplex. Repeat. Squash.
Squash. Repeat. Hundreds of days
as the WWE Universal Champion,
which apparently comes with a clause
that you can take a couple of months off,
no worries, no problem.

I'm just the asshole who didn't get why it mattered
that he was back, destroying everyone and everything.
Ending The Streak at WrestleMania.

Just
don't
get
it,
man,
or Vince,
or God,
or whoever's reading
this shit.

Another reason why I stopped watching
a lot of wrestling.

Once in a while, at the very least,
the current future of the industry
needs to surprise me a little.

Lose to someone in a shocking upset
(yes, nerds, yes,
I know Brock did this with Eddie Guerrero
in 2004, so you can be quiet now).

Start a tag team with Rick Steiner's mom.
Start a weird stable.
Start a detective agency.

I don't really give a shit.

WWE hasn't been very interesting to me
for a long time now.

Brock Lesner isn't solely to blame for this,
but when I talk about how boring wrestling
can be for me sometimes,
a hell of a distance from an age
where even WCW Thunder was entertaining,
The Beast's name inevitably comes up.

I'm sure he would be devastated
to hear of my disappointment.

Just crushed.

There Will Never Be a Trainwreck Quite Like TNA

Bizarre booking choices
that could make any wrestling fan
feel like someone just fucked your mom
and didn't even take you to IHOP
for uncomfortable pancakes.

Jeff Jarrett.
Jeff Jarrett.
Jeff Jarrett.
Jeff Jarrett?
Say the name to begin the fever dream.

The WCW Farewell Tour,
but there's also misfits like Ken Shamrock
and a bunch of indie talent who haven't turned the world
on fire quite yet.
That's coming up,
and if you're watching NWA Tits N Ass,
especially from its unfathomably surreal beginning,
it's going to be a little hard
to catch the brilliance sometimes.

Most amazing things
associated with Vince Russo
are amazing
in spite of Vince Russo.

I think it's important to remember that as we press on
and watch Russo shitting the bed so bad and so often,
it's a legitimate religious miracle that TNA survived, bro.

I don't think you should be allowed to like pro wrestling,
and calm down, nerds, because maybe I'm just kidding,
if you can't appreciate a good old-fashioned trainwreck
once in a while. Or every increasingly unhinged week
on PPV.

Wait, weekly PPVs?
Are you fucking serious?

Is Scott Hall sober for this?
Is anyone?

Six-sided rings.
Reverse battle royals.
Soap opera theatrics
that even Vince McMahon (well no probably not ha ha)
would be embarrassed by (nah, pal).

Hulk Hogan
pissing momentum down his leg
like it's a fetish.

But then you've got
Kurt Angle,
Sting,
AJ Styles,
and Christopher Daniels
turning in some of the best matches of their careers.

The surreal and terrible dominate this scene harder
than they do for the Vinegar Syndrome catalog,
but just like a drive-in running the 100 worst best movies

you've never heard of,
while deep south mutants "borrow" your eyes
and life-or-ego-death drinking contests
chase rubbing alcohol
with plastic bottle vodka
(what's the difference, really),
TNA had some amazing, crazed bits and astonishing bobs
that made the viewing experience a little more interesting.

And when the competition is doing the same thing
week after week, month after month,
and even if it's beautifully produced and sometimes
technically incredible,
you can put a premium on the chaotic and often godawful.

AJ Styles vs Christopher Daniels vs Samoa Joe
at Unbreakable 2005.
AMW vs Triple X at Turning Point 2004.
The Motor City Machine Guns against Beer Money
on free TV in 2010.

The worst stuff in wrestling is at least forgivable
if it's interesting, and if you take breaks
from testing the limits of human patience
with talent who will take any opportunity
to show you
some of the most incredible moments
you've ever seen in a wrestling ring.

It must be working on some level for TNA,
since they're still around after 20 years.

Outlasting their worst contributors,
an assortment of Presidents
and the most tedious social trends,
and even the Confederacy.
Anything that outlasts the Confederacy,
and features Scott Steiner Math,
Samoa Joe (that's it, just Samoa Joe)
and Kurt Angle, jacked on Percocet,
seemingly putting his actual life on the line
to get TNA over,
is worth celebrating if you ask me.

The Rowdy One, Forever

Roddy Piper was one of the real ones.

Whatever the fuck that even really means.

He was one of them.
An endlessly strange guy
with a distinctly unfortunate,
abusive childhood,
who committed himself
to wrestling with a fervor
he later found frightening and distasteful.

Not a lot of people are willing
to get hit by a car
at WrestleMania.

Or paint half their body black
to make a point about racism.
I think that needs to be a whole book unto itself,
because he certainly didn't make that choice clear
to Bad News Brown,
five-year-old Gabriel,
or anyone else in the world.

No one else called Mr. T and Hulk Hogan cowards,
or broke a coconut
over Jimmy Superfly Snuka's head,
and if you're feeling bad for Jimmy for some reason,
forty years later,

remember that Vince McMahon Jr
helped Jimmy beat a murder charge,
after the Superfly beat a woman to death,
so fuck Snuka anyway.

Roddy did it all,
good and bad,
as though it was the realest shit
you've ever seen,
and this includes Neil Breen-style promos
inside Alcatraz,
and matches with Hogan and Jerry Lawler
so profoundly terrible,
it's easier to pretend they've gone the way
of every Jerry Lewis Nazi clown movie
ever made.

No one asked Vince Russo
in front of a pay per view audience
if he killed Owen Hart.
Except Roddy Piper.
Maybe it was to do some good
business in his TNA debut,
but I want to doubt it.

When the fuck did Rowdy Roddy Piper
ever need anything
but himself
to get over.

And other rhetorical questions
we must ask
before Roddy changes them again.

And it turns out
we didn't have any of the answers after all.

Who was the greatest shit talker on the mic ever.

Who elevated the notion of screaming
at an arena full of desperate lunatics
and disenfranchised thrill-seekers
into its own wild artform.

Who was an okay wrestler
who nonetheless made me believe,
almost to the end of his life,
that he could dogfight his way out of anything.

Or at the very least,
make every moment
of his opponent's time in the ring
a living hell.

It took Hulk Hogan over a decade
to actually beat Roddy Piper.

Who was outstanding
in John Carpenter's They Live
and at least very memorable
in Hell Comes to Frogtown.

Who was at WrestleMania
when it didn't have a number.

Who beat the shit
out of Greg "The Hammer" Valentine

in a dog collar match
we're still watching and talking about.

I can go on like this
because just talking about
Rowdy Roddy Piper,
standing alone in life and death,
makes me feel like he's still here.

I want to go on.
I never really get tired of talking about
Rowdy Roddy Piper.

Who was truly a singular,
tough-as-nails performer
in the wrestling fan part of my life.

Right again.
Who is maybe the only wrestler
no one will ever be able to imitate.
Exactly.
Should you throw rocks at someone
who has a machine gun.
Ask Playboy Buddy Rose.

And His Opponent...

Weighing in tonight at 173 pounds!
From St. Louis, Missouri!

He is the founder of Back of the Class Press and author of *Snake Oil, Love Letters from the Underground,* and *Rodeo of the Soul*

He has been called the smartest drunk at three in the morning. The self-professed poet laureate of every gas station in the state of Missouri...

Damn right, it's Dan "The Man" Wright!!!!!

Introduction

Explaining my love for wrestling is one of the most difficult things I can think to do. That's why I love it when I meet another fan. You have an immediate shorthand with another person, and you can spend hours talking about favorite matches, wrestlers, debating on behind the scenes politics. Despite how many people go to shows and fill up arenas across the world, it still retains something of an outsider status. Maybe that's why punk rock and pro wrestling went so well together from almost day one when Dictators lead singer "Handsome" Dick Manitoba graced their first album's cover in his wrestling gear.

Though even those who are fellow outsiders may deride pro wrestling as an art form, like many other outsider art forms, it helped shape technology, was a main attraction for some towns as they were forming their identities, and gave fans hope when the world had kicked them a little harder that day. The only difference is while other outsider art forms eventually found cultural acceptance, there has always been something holding wrestling back. But for those who love it, there's nothing else like it.

It has been an honor working on this project with Gabe. Never has a project been as easy or as fun as this. In my experience, that's a definite sign of making something worthwhile.

For Mom and Jeff.

Guilty Pleasure

It's easier to bleed for your money
than it is
to sing for your supper
Even those who never watched
know the hustles
of the traveling circus days

It's hard to impress the high brows
when your sister is burlesque
and your friends
are jazz and comic books
You all started in the steerage
of the American Dream

Like all good American artforms
we embrace it
as much as we are embarrassed by it
When you understand
no excuse is necessary
When you don't want to understand
no excuse will do

Still Real to Me

Every month the circuit travels
catching the matches in VFW Halls,
school gymnasiums,
Athletic Clubs,
and wherever else that will have them
The fans who cheer tomorrow
Shows run by whatever bookers remain
from yesteryear.
Men who probably had
mob connections
at some point

They cheer the weekend warriors
and youthful prospects
Wearing camo hats
holding a can of Busch
Remembering the days of Ric Flair
and Wrestling at the Chase
Ride or die who still regard the NWA
as the gold standard
Who still bring pocket knives
just in case they get drunk enough
to think stabbing a wrestler
they don't like
is a good idea

They scream, "it's still real to me!"
Long after Athletic Commissions,
screwjobs,

curtain calls,
and dirt sheets
have all given us
a glimpse backstage

They'll be the first to do a favor,
first to buy a ticket,
first to buy the merch,
first to blow the champ,
first to help a new fan,
first to encourage someone
finding their way
Just don't ever tell them that it's fake
because that'll be the last thing you do

Heel Turn

Stanislaus Zbyszko held the title over his head
at 47 years old
while Wayne Munn lay dazed
Somewhere the Stetcher Brothers
were laughing behind closed doors
and the Gold Dust Trio
Ed Lewis, Toots Mondt, and Billy Sandow
scrambled to right a ship
aware that their greed
led to a screwjob
the likes of which
would light up a chatboard
100 years later

A month later
Zbyszko laid down for Joe Stetcher
to complete his end of the deal
The first true heel turn
in the business

Three years later Ed Lewis beat Stetcher
to get the belt back
for the last truly legitimate title change
but the Trio was no more
The damage had been done

Disputes over who was the real world champion
reigned for a decade
until the NWA came together

This whole matter has been reenacted
countless times
for entertainment
but the one time it was real
nobody knew any better

Von Erich Therapy

She sat in her apartment
holding her new baby
with her boyfriend gone
His whereabouts unknown
She turned on the tv
and saw a cute barefoot guy in tights
beating up a bearded guy in tights
with long flowing hair
who bore a resemblance
to her now former boyfriend

She imagined it was him
getting his ass beat six ways from Sunday
She kept watching to see
the cute barefoot guy
had two brothers
who were just as cute

When a friend offered to take her
to the matches
she entered the Sportatorium
a shy wallflower
and she left screaming
for the heads
of the Fabulous Freebirds

As her baby grew up
they both cheered the Von Erichs
and she smiled knowing her son
looked up to heroes
not villains

As the territories and heroes passed
she still watched whatever she could
always cheering for the heroes
because when bad people get away
with so much in the real world
it's good to see justice
prevail somewhere
even if it's only in a wrestling ring

Earn Your Stripes

Doing wheelbarrows with a partner
up and down thirty flights of stairs
five days a week
before learning sound fundamentals
Running for miles until you throw up
training in a barn
in the dead of winter
A veteran breaking someone's leg
on the first day of training
to see if they'll come back
Being stretched to your limit
your body being contorted in ways
you didn't know it could
as you scream bloody murder

Sending a kid in to fetch some snacks
only to leave him at the gas station
three hundred miles from the venue
Dressing outside the locker room
because the veterans have said
you haven't earned the right

Blindfolded and bound
letting the locker room take turns
kicking your privates
Taking liberties with someone in the ring
to see if they can hack it
and ask for more

Being hit with a kendo stick
across the back
in front of a crowd
until your back is bruised
beyond belief

This life ain't for the weak
But once you're in
you're in for life

Get the Match in the Ring

It doesn't matter
what their ego wants
How big a deal
they think they are
Just get the match in the ring
send the folks home happy
Then you can deal
with consequences and actions

They don't see the deals in the office,
the shakedowns from people higher up
The cut
that people of means
want to take
when they see
you've worked hard
to be successful

The fact that the buck
has to stop somewhere
if you want to be looked upon
with respect
But with respect from some
comes hatred from others
The road to success
is paved with broken promises
and broken bodies

Other promoters plotting to kill you
because you approached the inevitable
before they did

Wrestlers holding you up
refusing to go to the ring
unless they are guaranteed
more money

With bigger business
comes bigger challenges
because nothing in this world is free
But no matter the problem
no matter the headache
whatever happens
just get the match in the ring
Everything else can be dealt with later

Walk That Aisle

When you walk that aisle
WOOO!
wearing custom robes
that cost $3,000 a pop
with hair that's perfect
to go an hour
in the main event
WOOOOO!
Driving a Lincoln Continental
to the arena
and arriving
wearing a custom made suit
WOOOOOOOOO!
with $600 alligator shoes
and a Rolex watch
With men and women lined up at the door
to shake hands with you
and to touch
the World Heavyweight Championship belt
WOOOOOOOOOOOOOOOO!
To be in the presence of greatness
To see the best damn wrestler
who never has a day off
To travel from Toronto
to Charlotte
to Mobile
to Kansas City
to St. Louis
and back to KC for one week

Then a week in Texas
Then a week in Atlanta
Then a week in Florida
and a week in Puerto Rico
where you got stabbed last time
you were in town
because you went over
on their top hero
Then Los Angeles
to San Francisco
to Seattle
to Las Vegas
to Phoenix
and still deliver
five-star match
after five-star match
WWOOOOOOOOOOOOOOO!
To live up to the reputation of being
the stylin', profilin', limousine riding,
jet flying, kiss-stealing,
wheelin' and dealin'
son of a gun

Proclaiming to everyone
daring to climb that mountain
that to be the man,
you gotta beat the man!
WOOOOOOOOOOOOOOOOOOOOO!!!!!
To hear the knife edge chops
WOO!
Delivered to an opponent
every night

and finishing them all off
with the figure four leglock
for the win
to still hold on to that world title
with a tear in your eye
WWWWOOOOOOOOOOOOOOOOOOOOOOO!!!
And then to go to the nearest bar
where the drinks are all on the champ tonight
As party time is on all night long

*WWWWWWOOOOOOOOOOOOOOOOOOOO
OOOOOOOO!!!!!!!!!!!!!!!!!*

Space Mountain
may be the oldest ride
but it still has the longest line
Living life on a razor's edge
waking a mess
but ending immaculate
and doing it all over again
the next day
because diamonds are forever
and so are you

Hailing from Parts Unknown

Home to missing links
voodoo priests
demons
and warriors
of the ultimate kind

It is a hellscape like no other
a faraway land
beyond the deepest jungles
and deadliest valleys
where identity is hidden

Where some are born with mist
they can spray upon an opponent
Green to obstruct vision
Red to burn the eyes
Black to blind them
Blue to send them to sleep

Some call it the fifth dimension
or the outer reaches of your mind
Satanic worship is revered
magic is commonplace
No one has been able to find
this strange place
and those who leave
can never find their way back

The Battle of the Bite

To agree to a fight
on enemy turf
is always a bad decision
You know the fix is in
But sometimes in order to do business
you have no other choice
save for giving a son of a bitch
the opportunity
to make you a son of a bitch

Two out of three falls
with the first fall going as planned
in Montreal, 1931
The second fall ends in disqualification
with the champ losing the two falls
a new champion crowned
from a rival promotion
claiming the champ bit him
while many speculate
the challenger's manager
bit him hard enough
to draw blood
in the locker room
after the first fall
to look legit for the official

Sixty-six years later
another wrestling screwjob
would happen in Montreal

Just as the first go around
many speculated
it was a work
something to pull over
on the fans
but everyone involved
always swore
it was real

Road Warriors

When you've been knocked down,
dragged every which way
fish hooked and had your eyes gouged
hips are counting down
how much longer they've got
and you know the rats are waiting
200 miles down the road
with the promise of a good time

When you've spent twenty seven days
away from your family
and the only people to commiserate with
besides the guys you share a ride with
is the 2 pm stripper
who has been at her hustle
as long as you have been at yours
You realize that the only thing that's real
is the money
and the miles

No Holds Barred Grudge Match

Like anything else
it has to start small
and grow as wild and free
as it is meant to
It could be about money
or opportunity
or a girl
or even something as simple
as just plain not liking someone else

Both sides talk the talk
They interfere with the day to day lives
of each other
They'll have a match
that ends without a decisive winner
A personal attack is made
and met with equal retaliation
Maybe an injury of a friend
or one of the warring parties
Blood is spilt
Words are uttered
that cut deep

The audience knows
that the there is only one way
this ends
In a cage or with no disqualification
In a match that will no doubt
change those going into this match
And if it's done right
both sides will be better for it

Austin vs McMahon

"Is this going to really happen?"
was all my almost fourteen year old brain
could think
as I saw 52 year old Vince McMahon
the owner of the World Wrestling Federation
who had never entered a ring before
as a competitor
walk down to the ring
with his yes men in tow

Quickly after McMahon entered the ring
his son Shane came down
to try and talk his father
out of going through
with this match

And then the sound of the glass shattering
got the crowd in a frenzy
as Stone Cold Steve Austin's theme
blared in the arena
as the newly crowned WWF World Champion
came out
And as Austin shoulder-checked McMahon
while making his way to a ring corner
to pose for the fans
I kept thinking,
"Is this REALLY gonna happen?!"

And then
as the two stared each other down
McMahon slapped Austin across the face
and I got in trouble
because I yelled,
"Holy shit! This is REALLY gonna HAPPEN!"

But before things began
McMahon reminded Austin
that earlier in the night
when the challenge was made
that Austin said he could beat Vince
with one arm tied behind his back

With Austin's arm tied behind his back
the two were moving toward each other
and I thought
this was ACTUALLY GONNA HAPPEN
Dude Love came out
to break up the fight
and wound up attacking Steve Austin
and as McMahon left the ring
I realized that the match
wasn't gonna happen

But for ten minutes
they had over five million people hooked
to their television screens
thinking they were going to see
what was then
the impossible

Thunderlips

He'll tell you
that Andre the Giant died
days after their WrestleMania III encounter
despite Andre living another six years
He'll tell you
he was the original bassist for Metallica
even though the band has said
they have never met the man
and he was already a top star
in another part of the world

He claims he fought Pride Fighters
in the 1970s
although Pride was not formed
until 1997
He'll spin a tale
for those too young to know
that he fought Mike Tyson
and George Foreman
Maybe my Millennial brain is fading
because I don't seem to recall that
and neither does any history book
He'll tell any fan willing to listen
that he met Elvis
long after the King was dead
That he played AAA ball
despite no records existing

He messes with the boys in the back
telling an up-and-comer
that they were unsafe in the ring with him
even as there is video evidence
of them being as safe as possible
He'll agree to the demands of the boss
to help the company pass the torch
only to turn around and say,
"It doesn't work for me brother."

Ride an angle as a top villain
straight to the bank
only to back out of the inevitable ending
losing clean to the chosen hero
by claiming the hero
isn't tan enough
to look enough like a hero
to the people
Whatever that means

He'll screw over his comrades
and futures wrestlers
by squashing any hopes of a union
just so he can make the top money
Demand that his contract include a percentage
of all merch sales
be they his or others'
Creative control is a make or break deal
with b-movie films
he will tell you he wrote

He'll infuriate a former best friend
so much
that they'll write a rap album
with the title track
calling him out to a fight
There'll be a rumor
that the former best friend
left a black eye
seen on pay-per-view
that was blamed on a jet ski

He'll claim the accolades of others
to look good
because the hustle
is never over
so long as he's breathing

And he'll also try to tell you
that he never used steroids in his life
but everyone knows
that's a crock of shit

Charlie Brown from Outta Town

When evil triumphs over good
and sends them outta town
a masked man
will ride into town
maybe to the theme of the Lone Ranger
bearing a slight resemblance
to someone who is no longer around
to continue fighting the good fight.

They will wear a mask
over another mask
to protect their identity
to make sure evil never gets
the upper hand

They will stand up for what is true
making friends with everyone
the beloved hero
was once friends with
The most they will claim
was that they were a fan
of the cast out hero
and only want to fight
for their return

And when the hero inevitably returns
they will thank
Charlie Brown
from outta town

who conveniently
rode off into the sunset
to fight the good fight

Satanic Sunshine

The misunderstood
are often the ones
capable of the most evil
Doing what's necessary
to win a title
makes others proclaim
you're not the same man anymore

Taking a Satanic panic
and making it your plaything
Praying in gibberish
while mothers cry
thinking their sons have sold their souls
by playing Dungeons and Dragons
or listening to heavy metal
Appearing on television
wearing face paint
under the eyes
and an X
in the middle of your forehead

Convincing others to see your way
leading them in an army of darkness
Telling them to retire from life
and be born again under your tutelage
People around the state
running in fear
claiming they saw you
at the store

in Satanic garb
wearing a hood and a dog collar

Fighting a legend
in a one-week fight
Never declaring
Satan is your manager
but one headline is all it takes
for people to believe

Mentions of golden palms
and cosmic cookies
all it takes
for ringside crowds
to ask the Lord to save them
from the evil
that stands in front of them

Eleven Hours to Oklahoma City

After entertaining a sold out crowd
for three to five hours
a group of thirty to forty men
in the dead of night
bruised, bloody, and beaten
have to haul ass from New Orleans
back to Oklahoma City
for live television the next day
before starting the trek
all over again
from Oklahoma City to New Orleans
throughout the week
to haul ass back
for television the next day

A passion never promised
to make any sense

Black Star

The second you take liberties
with someone
who has trusted you
with their body
Go into business for yourself
for whatever reason
you can not be trusted
Trust is what keeps
any performing art alive

No matter the reason
no matter the excuse
popping an arm
out of its socket
in front of a live crowd
at a company's biggest event
of the year
can never be undone

When all you have
in a shark tank
is trust
Breaking your word
is one thing
but breaking a body
is something else

Acknowledge Him

Over 1,000 days as world champion
means you must acknowledge
your Tribal Chief
From one of the greatest wrestling families
in the history of the business
who have never faltered
and have given respect back to an industry
that has treated them well

Four generations
from the Wild Samoans
to the Rock
and beyond
When your Tribal Chief
graces you with his presence
along with the rest of the Bloodline
stand up and listen
when he says,
"Acknowledge me"

Million Dollar Body and a Ten Cent Brain

They'll look good in the ring
but usually can't wrestle for shit
They'll stumble around
while a more seasoned vet
tries to make them look good
or if the body has a bad attitude
the vet may reach their limit
and run circles
around the godlike specimen
and expose this million dollar body
for not being worth
its appraisal

They'll be gone
in a few years
making the quick cash
they got in the business for
Becoming a memory
with diminished returns

Because while it is wiser
to make a lot of money
over a lot of years
with the best talent
most promoters
only want to make
a lot of cash upfront
not thinking
about the possibility
of long-term booking

This Television Thing is Here to Stay

On a cold winter's night
February 21st, 1947
an experimental new thing
called television
broadcast the first world heavyweight
championship title change
as Whipper Billy Watson won
the National Wrestling Association
World title
in St. Louis, MO
on KSD-TV

At most
maybe 500 people
got to see the match
on a television screen
with the experiment proving a success
and the potential for the technology
proving unlimited

Some dared to claim
that maybe one day
the device could broadcast images
in lifelike color
While others wished
there could have been a way
for Watson's hometown
of Toronto
to have seen the match

Hitting That Sweet Spot

Pain becomes secondary
Time moves differently
You forget what was discussed
yet you know everything to do
and run purely on instinct

To feel the roar of the crowd
as you know you have them
right in the palm of your hand
The fans feel far away
as tunnel vision takes hold
and right next to you
as you ride the wave
they are giving you

No second guesses tonight
until you snap out of the trance
you've been in
With any luck
the come down happens backstage
and the boys will tell you
everything looked great
and your dance partner is happy
with how it went down

You may watch it on a monitor after
with your memory giving you
flashes of remembrance
It doesn't happen too often

But with the right combination
of crowd, opponent, hype, and an unknown else
you hit the sweet spot
every performer longs to reach

A Night with Mad Dog

Superhuman strength
and superhuman stupidity
lay at the feet
of a dozen bottles
We all go off the rails
sometimes
and we all feel like shit
the day after
with a night's worth of regrets

But until you drink
a pint of whiskey
before entertaining a crowd
for twenty minutes
Downed two Dexedrine
with an entire cooler of beer
in thirty minutes
Emptied three bottles of red wine
to calm your nerves
before meeting your girlfriend's parents
for the first time
Drank another full bottle of whiskey
after embarrassing yourself
in front of your girlfriend and her parents
and then smoked a joint to even out
because you drank too much
and took a quaalude
to calm down because the joint didn't hit
like you thought it would
before getting on a plane
to go home

Until you have opened up the door
of a plane 10,000 feet in the air,
throwing your friends' gym bags out
and yelling to your friends
as you hang out the door
of the plane
"I tell ya, it's so peaceful up here,
I feel like I'm flying"

Until you have fought
six of your best friends
all of whom are in much better shape
than you'll ever be
after the plane has landed
and at least seven cops
and a few men from the local psych ward
ready to put you in a straight jacket
screaming at everyone
as the cops ask your friends
if they want to press charges
"I swear I'll take you all to Hell with me!"
and your friends instead deciding
to go to a local hardware store
Buy a shit ton of duct tape
and tape you to your seat
before the plane takes off again
and leave you tied up
after the plane lands
for the pilots to deal with you

Until you've had a night like that
Don't beat yourself up too bad

The Hot Tag

Two men walk down the aisle
wearing matching gear
sometimes with a manager
too outspoken for their own good
Sometimes it's two good looking guys
blasting rock n' roll to the rafters
Other times it's two towering behemoths
who look like they could turn you
into their own personal hand puppet

Tagging with someone
is a whole different ballgame
than just facing someone one-on-one
But like any art
when it's done right
the crowd goes crazy

Quick tags help a team
cut off the ring
wearing down one of their opponents
While their partner is left
chomping at the bit
to become the legal man
and clean house

Some promoters may not care much
for the style
but sometimes the best kind of fight
is one where you know

your best friend
has got your back

That is until the sudden and inevitable betrayal
that seems to befall most teams
sooner or later.

Mark Them

If anyone tries you tonight
mark them
Break a rib
Break an arm
leave a bruise somewhere
they can't hide
Gouge an eye out

If they wanna start a fight
because they recognize a wrestler
they saw on tv
then it's your job to make them bleed
I don't care if you wind up in jail
I'll post bail
Just make sure you mark them
before the fight gets broken up
Something that will be a reminder
to think twice
before doing that again
for at least a few weeks

Because they're gonna have a story to tell
about how they fought a wrestler
and got their ass kicked
Then their friends will know
that everything else might be planned
but that one wrestler
HE'S REAL!

And if you wind up
getting your ass kicked
don't bother coming in tomorrow
because you're done
in this territory

Elegy for Frank Goodish

No one knows what happened
but everybody knows what happened
Deals go wrong
with people who speak their mind
Another example of when keeping it real
goes wrong
Screams were heard
some say they saw a bloody knife

The murderer acquitted
on grounds of self defense
with summons for key witnesses
being delivered ten days
after the trial had ended

With a rep of working stiff
and scared of no man
he scared the hell out of fans
and wrestlers alike

Some called him King Kong
Some called him Bruiser
But when he walked
through that curtain
everyone called him Brody

Backyard Badasses

At first glance,
this looks like a bad audition tape
for Jackass
Most of the time you can see
a swing set in the background
with a slide usually in shot

The wanna be wrestlers
make their entrance
via the back door
looking like tenth rate
second generation
Slim Shadys

Lawnchairs are set up
for the few friends who show up
to cheer their friends on
Most matches
become hardcore matches
with someone falling off the roof
and into a table spot

If this burgeoning indie fed
has any money they may pay ICP
to make an appearance
and fight whatever makeshift
tag team champions
the company has at the moment

No one is trained
and very few ever try
to go legit
but they feel part
of the wrestling family
where so many
already feel like orphans

Didn't They Used to…

Anything that happened three months ago
can be forgotten
Anything that happened seven years ago
can happen again
The ref will get knocked out
once again
The same friend will turn their back
on the same hero
with the hero just as shocked as they were
the first time around

A psychotic dentist
can become the Devil's favorite demon
A people's champion
can become a crazed stalker
and a millionaire playboy
can become a gladiator named Spartacus
All in the name of getting over
Whatever can put
butts in the seats

And since everyone on screen
has the memory of a fish
they expect the same
from their audience
to varying results

The Many Sins of Vince McMahon

Nancy Argentino lies dead
her death swept under the rug
with rumors that Pennsylvania police
received a pay-off
to not look into matters
because her boyfriend
Superfly Jimmy Snuka
was the biggest star in the company

The stories of sexual assault
against a minor named Tom Cole
and the first female referee
Rita Marie Chatterton
are still not known by many

Making an announcer's bell's palsy
a punchline
A plane ride from hell labeled
as just "boys being boys"
Forcing talent to engage
in a "live sex celebration"
on Monday night live television
or else they would be fired
While laughing
as a son-in-law simulates
necrophilia

Taking every deal
honored by a father

for almost fifty years
and flushing it down the toilet
in the name of business
Leaving talent to be regarded
as "independent contractors"
but not allowing them
to work anywhere else

Wishing employees well
in future endeavors
by mailing talent
their personal items
in a trash bag
Letting talent go
because you're "cutting costs"
despite making record profits

Screwing over a loyal employee
of fifteen years
live on pay-per-view
after telling that employee
to get a better deal
because a guarantee
could not be fulfilled
And eighteen months later
that now former employee's brother
falls to his death
in front
of a live pay-per-view crowd
because he didn't like the idea
of portraying himself
as having an affair

and didn't want his wife dragged on to TV
to pretend
one of the worst things
a person can go through

With 16,472 fans in Kansas City
watching that man
fall eighty feet in the air
His last words yelling at a ref
to get out of the way
because he didn't want that ref
to get hurt
His head hitting the turnbuckle
and snapping back
And none
of those 16,472 fans are questioned
by the police
as the show goes on

Pitching an idea
where you are revealed
to be having gotten your own daughter
pregnant
and not understanding
why everyone involved
would feel uncomfortable
by such an idea

He took the blood
of those who worked for him
and built Titan Towers

He took their dreams
and bought himself a private jet
He took their smiles
and took his company public
It's all about the money
Complaining that men aren't men anymore
while hiring underwear models
and teaching them how to wrestle
because it looks good on television.

Another great American success story
With all the details in the fine print
No one pays attention
except for the fans
And if you were to ask Vince
about the controversy
the pain
and the ratings
he'd say,
"It's such good shit, pal!"

A Higher Tolerance

When you're 7'4"
and 520 pounds
it takes a little more
than three or four cans of beer
for you to feel anything
In fact it's closer to 119 cans
in six hours

Drinking an entire plane dry
with Ric Flair
or running up a $40,000 tab
one night in 1987

Drinking an entire case of wine
in three hours
to pass the time on a bus
as you make the next town

Or forty vodka tonics
'til four in the morning
long after the bar is closed
because no one wants to tell
a drunken giant
its time to leave

The Scaffold Match or Fuck That Shit, You're Not Getting My Ass Up There

Twenty-five feet in the air
a scaffold is placed over the ring
with either two wrestlers
or two tag teams
scaling the scaffold
to get up to the top
to fight each other
with the purpose of the match
being to throw your opponent
or opponents
off the scaffold

Sometimes there are tables
set up in the ring
to help break a fall
Other times
all that's left
is to pray while you fall
that you'll survive
and not be injured
for months on end

Whoever is getting tossed
off the scaffold
gets extra pay in their check
that night
and a booker asking
if they'd be up

for doing it again
considering all the money
they brought in from this match
with most of that extra money
the losing side received
probably going to hospital bills

Blind Man with a Gun

Leroy McGuirk had been blind
since a car accident in 1950
in Little Rock
took his sight
but that still didn't stop him
from being in a business he loved

One day in 1974
now a promoter
McGuirk heard that one of the wrestlers
working for him
had begun dating his daughter
which he thought
was a sin against humanity
So McGuirk thought
the only logical solution
was to take his .44
and shoot that wrestler

Knowing he needed help
in knowing where to shoot
on the car ride to the arena
McGuirk asked his college aged assistant
to become an accomplice
and point out the wrestler
whenever the assistant saw him

Not wanting to go to jail
the assistant called McGuirk's boss

from a payphone
and explained the whole situation
The boss showed up
and kept McGuirk in his hotel room
while the show went on that night
because the wrestling world
can explain away
a lot of things
Homicide isn't one of them

Harley Race vs the Hell's Angel

While wrestling one night in Oregon
the eight-time NWA World Heavyweight Champion
Harley Race
was heckled by a group
in the front row
that turned out to be
a bunch of Hell's Angels

After the matches
the bikers waited
for Race to come out
When Harley saw the bikers
waiting for him
he went up
to the biggest one of the group
headbutted the man in the nose,
turned him around,
and put him in a sleeper hold
while a river of blood
dripped down from the man's nose

The rest of the bikers backed off
seeing their comrade passed out
with some thinking
he was dead
Harley Race enjoyed the rest of his night
in peace

Robocop Saves the Day

As Sting was put in a cage
in the ringside area
by the Four Horsemen
The crowd hoped
for any friend of the Stinger
to come down
and save Sting
from the most dastardly group
WCW had ever known

Maybe the Road Warriors
or the Rock n' Roll Express
Maybe the Steiner Brothers
or Brian Pillman and Tom Zenk
all of whom
were scheduled on the show
and all of whom
had issues with the Horsemen
in the past

But a force of good
much greater
than any mere wrestler
came out to save Sting
from the metal cage
with rubber bars

It was Robocop
straight from Detroit

and a new movie
Making his way down to ringside
with his plastic armor
barely staying on

He didn't throw a punch
he couldn't get physical
but the mere presence
of Robocop
sent the Horsemen
running for their lives

Later in the main event
as Ric Flair faced Lex Luger
in a steel cage
and the Horsemen came down
to help their leader
and Sting came down
to help Luger
it would have been normal
to assume
that Robocop would have reappeared
to help good
triumph over evil
But he did not

I guess Robocop
is just another cop
you can't trust

Oh, I Knew That Guy

Growing up in the same suburban area
as the Orton family
I heard all the time
about Cowboy Bob Orton
and which car dealership
he worked at

When Randy Orton made the main roster
I heard from every Taco Bell
and Blockbuster employee
who looked like they ain't seen pussy
since pussy saw them
that they all kicked Randy's ass
when he was younger

Some bragged
about hooking up with his sister
as though that honor
brought them closer
to a fame they resigned themselves
to never knowing

But everyone agreed
from passing acquaintances
 to people who claimed to be
former best friends
he was an asshole
but they still wished him well

Fear and Loathing in a Dairy Queen Drive-Thru

In a Kentucky town
that ain't big enough
to have a McDonald's
The only thing open late for fast food
where everyone wants to go
on a Saturday night
is a Dairy Queen

When you've waited twenty minutes for food
and they haven't started making it
because they didn't think an order that big
would be real
When a booker
with an already short fuse
loses his temper
on a slave to minimum wage
as a few wrestlers inside
hear their boss
screaming from the drive thru window

It's just another day in the circus
Another moment of surreal reality
that no drug could have ever
prepared you for
But someone in the car
was able to capture it all
on a camcorder
because no words
could ever do it justice

Memories of a Modern Wrestling Fan from St. Louis

St. Louis has always been
one of the best wrestling cities
Not that I'm biased or anything
I may have never seen Wild Bill Longson
sell out crowds
of tens of thousands
or been able to applaud
when Lou Thesz got his hand raised
but am proud to say
I shook hands with Harley Race

I may never have been able
to go to a show promoted by Sam Muchnick
but I have seen Kane make his debut
ripping the door off the Hell in a Cell
I was grounded for a week
when the Rock cheated Mankind
to regain the WWF title
and I exclaimed in front of my mom,
"That's a bunch of bullshit!"
In one month
I cheered
when Kevin Nash defeated DDP
for the WCW world championship
at the Trans World Dome
and paid my respects to Owen Hart
at the Keil Center

With my brother beside me
I saw Cody Rhodes and Goldust
defeat the Shield for the tag titles
We couldn't believe our eyes
when we saw Sting make his debut with the WWE
I have talked about my love of the business
with Larry Matisyk
Heard stories from those older than me
about going to Wrestling at the Chase

Bronze age memories may mean nothing
to those who were there
during the golden or silver age
But they mean everything
to those young enough to be moved
by what they saw
And at the end of the day,
Isn't that what it's all about

The Bucks Gotta Stop Somewhere

How hard can it be
are famous last words
for anyone diving head first
into a world
they don't understand

No boss ever got respect
by trying to befriend his workers
Working hard to gain their approval
whilst being the one
signing the paychecks

Chasing away every bit of legitimacy
for the sake of making someone happy
who is only using someone
with an endless bank account
is not a good business plan
The buck's gotta stop somewhere
but it won't ever stop
with the Michael Scott
of the wrestling world

Got Your Nose

If the stories are to be believed
Chuck Norris and Brock Lesnar
live in fear of Meng
who some may also know as Haku
He was once maced by police,
handcuffed,
and then broke the cuffs
without breaking a sweat

Some have said he was one of two men
that made even Andre the Giant
think twice
before starting shit
That he once pushed a 6'5" cowboy
through two different sets of doors
using only one hand
That he lifted Brutus Beefcake
by the neck
off the ground
after hearing Beefcake talk shit after a match

Rumor has it
he took a man's eye out
for kicking dirt on a man
and that once in a bar
a man tried staring a fight with him
and with just two fingers
index and trigger
he reached in the guy's mouth
and broke off the guy's bottom teeth

One of the few stories he confirmed
was once in the Baltimore Airport
he was asked
if he was "one of those fake wrestlers"
to which he responded
by biting the man's nose off

When asked later about it
he said he had no regrets

Dedicated to the Memory of Katie Vick

Wrestling fans deal with a lot
We take shit for something we enjoy
from people who don't understand
and we have to repeatedly cough
and turn the other way
when the people producing wrestling shows
insult our intelligence
in a stream of endless possibilities

But when the WWE introduced a storyline
with simulated necrophilia
that was the moment
my brother and I turned to each other
and decided
to change the channel

Within moments of the segment
that culminated with the line,
"I guess I fucked your brains out"
every wrestling fan with a keyboard
said what my brother and I were thinking

Most of us eventually came back
because at the time
there weren't many other options
But even older wrestling fans
had some remaining innocence
taken from them
after watching that

It's like when a friend
has a sick joke
that you don't want to hear
but they tell it anyway
Sooner or later
you don't want to hang out
with that friend anymore

Exit Light, Enter Night

At an ECW show in Milwaukee
a wrestler known as Rhino
showed up late in tears
telling his friend Tommy Dreamer
that their friend
Sandman
was dead
Rhino said that Sandman
had injected Nubain
and had OD'd in the car
Rhino and the others in the car,
Quickly got rid
of the rest of the drugs in the car
and then dropped off Sandman's body
at the nearest hospital
telling the hospital staff,
"We just found this guy like this."

At the hospital
a shot of adrenaline
revived the Sandman
and he left the hospital
to make it to the show
and entertain the crowd
with his Metallica entrance music
and wrestle a match
before going to wherever the afterparty
was that night

Hate's a Hell of Motivator

When you have given your life
to an art
to a lifestyle
the last thing you want to see
is some asshole come in
and strip it for parts

To see respected friends
be crushed underneath bullshit
all because the top of a pyramid
got the wool pulled
over their eyes

To give sound warnings
only to be compared to Chicken Little
only to be proven right
with the passage of time
after everyone realizes
they were taken for a ride

To know that this life
that has given so much to you
and that you wanted to do right by
will never be the same again
because a con won out

Leaving the only option
to get back at that person
that you have grown to hate so much

being for you to live a healthy life
so you can outlive that con artist
and piss on their grave

It may not be
the healthiest way to live
but hate is a hell of a motivator
And if you can't brighten up
the entire world
you can at least brighten up
your part of it

When the Well Runs Dry

Progress can be magic
and progress can be death
Checks and balances can be thrown off
if everyone doesn't keep up
But sooner or later the well runs dry
and ten years on
the same talent doesn't excite
like they used to

And those who want to break in
don't know where to go
to learn their craft
so they can be ready
for the big stage
Because the path of success
everyone has been told to follow
was taken out
with no notice
before a new way
was put up

When old men don't want
to hand the reigns over
the old guard crumbles
ready for the new guard
to take over

But just because
you went with progress in your youth
doesn't mean

you can stop following progress
in old age

Another Monday Night

A blank check
Doesn't guarantee victory
It certainly helps
but people will always lean
towards a story they can relate to
that they maybe have already heard
a million times over
but will love to see it
told in a way
they've never seen before

Every tale is as old as time
And most people
have lived a couple of them
Give someone a reason
to believe in a hero
a reason to hate a villain
and they will be all in on a story

People will always cheer Rocky
They will always boo Emperor Palpatine
And if a story is told well enough
without any swerves
for the sake of a swerve
you can make anyone paying attention cry
when good triumphs over evil

The Sickness

We're never supposed to get older
but we all do
We never imagine
the day will finally come
to ride into the sunset
to hang up a lifetime's work
Hip replacements and calloused skin
with old war stories of those
long since gone
by tragic fate

As long as we breathe
we can work
What else can a warrior do
when all they know is to fight
When you have felt
the most addictive drug of them all
Hundreds
Thousands
Millions of people
screaming your name
Where is the detox from that
There's always one more fight
one more day
One more chance
to get the crowd going
and send them home happy

Gabriel Ricard writes, edits, and occasionally acts. He writes a monthly column called *Captain Canada's Movie Rodeo at Drunk Monkeys*, as well as a monthly column called *Make the Case with Cultured Vultures*. His newest book, *A Ludicrous Split 2* with Kevin Ridgeway, was published in April 2023 through Back of the Class Press. His 2015 poetry collection *Clouds of Hungry Dogs* is available from Kleft Jaw Press, while his 2017 novel *Bondage Night* is available through Moran Press. Recent releases include *A Ludicrous Split*, (Alien Buddha Press/Split chapbook with Kevin Ridgeway), and *Love and Quarters*, (Moran Press). Gabriel currently lives in Orlando, FL with his wife, three crazed ferrets, and an inability to stop ordering delivery. He watches way too many movies, has spent tens of thousands of miles on Greyhound, and has somehow also worked, or tried to, in fields such as radio, theater, and standup.

Daniel W. Wright is a poet, editor, and fiction writer. He is the co-founder of Back of the Class Press. Wright most recently released *From Obscurity to Oblivion: Collected Poems 2008-2017* (Spartan Press, 2022) and wrote the foreword for *Sacred Decay: The Art of Lauren Marx* (Dark Horse, 2021). He is the author of five collections of poetry and one collection of prose. His work has appeared in numerous print and online journals. Wright currently resides in St. Louis, MO, where you can usually find him in a bar or a bookstore.

This project was made possible, in part, by generous support from the Osage Arts Community.

Osage Arts Community provides temporary time, space and support for the creation of new artistic works in a retreat format, serving creative people of all kinds — visual artists, composers, poets, fiction and nonfiction writers. Located on a 152-acre farm in an isolated rural mountainside setting in Central Missouri and bordered by ¾ of a mile of the Gasconade River, OAC provides residencies to those working alone, as well as welcoming collaborative teams, offering living space and workspace in a country environment to emerging and mid-career artists. For more information, visit us at www.osageac.org

Osage Arts Community